50 International Smoothie Dishes for Home

By: Kelly Johnson

Table of Contents

- Brazilian Açaí Berry Smoothie
- Indian Mango Lassi Smoothie
- Mexican Horchata Smoothie
- Greek Yogurt Honey and Fig Smoothie
- Japanese Matcha Green Tea Smoothie
- Caribbean Coconut Pineapple Smoothie
- Thai Mango Coconut Smoothie
- Peruvian Lucuma Smoothie
- Moroccan Orange and Date Smoothie
- Italian Tiramisu Dessert Smoothie
- Turkish Apricot and Almond Smoothie
- Korean Banana Milk Smoothie
- French Lavender Blueberry Smoothie
- Hawaiian Tropical Papaya Smoothie
- Spanish Almond Horchata Smoothie
- Argentinian Dulce de Leche Smoothie
- Vietnamese Avocado Smoothie
- Swedish Lingonberry Smoothie
- Ethiopian Spiced Honey Smoothie
- Lebanese Rosewater Pistachio Smoothie
- Australian Beetroot and Carrot Smoothie
- Filipino Ube (Purple Yam) Smoothie
- Chinese Lychee and Ginger Smoothie
- Russian Kefir Berry Smoothie
- South African Rooibos Tea Smoothie
- Indonesian Tamarind and Coconut Smoothie
- Malaysian Pandan and Coconut Smoothie
- Middle Eastern Date and Cardamom Smoothie
- Colombian Passion Fruit Smoothie
- Swiss Chocolate Hazelnut Smoothie
- Chilean Guava Smoothie
- Polynesian Pineapple and Banana Smoothie
- Danish Apple and Oat Smoothie
- Finnish Cloudberry Smoothie
- Indian Spiced Chai Smoothie

- Tahitian Vanilla Coconut Smoothie
- Irish Cream and Coffee Smoothie
- Jamaican Sorrel (Hibiscus) Smoothie
- Pakistani Almond and Saffron Smoothie
- Ecuadorian Naranjilla Smoothie
- Icelandic Skyr Blueberry Smoothie
- Cuban Guava and Cheese Smoothie
- Nigerian Zobo (Hibiscus) Smoothie
- Alaskan Wildberry Smoothie
- Canadian Maple Apple Smoothie
- Hungarian Sour Cherry Smoothie
- Korean Sweet Potato Smoothie
- Venezuelan Papelon con Limón Smoothie
- Balinese Turmeric and Tamarind Smoothie
- Puerto Rican Pina Colada Smoothie

Brazilian Açaí Berry Smoothie

Ingredients:

- 1 frozen açaí puree pack
- 1 banana
- 1/2 cup frozen mixed berries
- 1/2 cup almond milk
- 1 tbsp honey (optional)

Instructions:

1. Blend all ingredients until smooth.
2. Pour into a glass and enjoy!

Indian Mango Lassi Smoothie

Ingredients:

- 1 cup ripe mango chunks
- 1/2 cup plain yogurt
- 1/4 cup milk
- 1 tbsp sugar or honey
- 1/4 tsp ground cardamom

Instructions:

1. Blend all ingredients until creamy.
2. Serve chilled, garnished with a pinch of cardamom.

Mexican Horchata Smoothie

Ingredients:

- 1/2 cup cooked white rice
- 1/2 cup almond milk
- 1/4 cup evaporated milk
- 1/2 tsp ground cinnamon
- 1 tbsp sugar or honey
- Ice cubes

Instructions:

1. Blend all ingredients until smooth.
2. Garnish with a cinnamon stick or dusting of cinnamon.

Greek Yogurt Honey and Fig Smoothie

Ingredients:

- 1/2 cup plain Greek yogurt
- 3 fresh figs (or dried, soaked figs)
- 1/4 cup almond milk
- 1 tbsp honey
- Ice cubes

Instructions:

1. Blend all ingredients until creamy.
2. Serve topped with a drizzle of honey.

Japanese Matcha Green Tea Smoothie

Ingredients:

- 1 tsp matcha powder
- 1/2 cup unsweetened almond milk
- 1 frozen banana
- 1/4 cup plain yogurt
- 1 tsp honey

Instructions:

1. Blend all ingredients until smooth.
2. Serve with a sprinkle of matcha powder.

Caribbean Coconut Pineapple Smoothie

Ingredients:

- 1 cup fresh or frozen pineapple chunks
- 1/2 cup coconut milk
- 1/4 cup orange juice
- 1/4 cup shredded coconut
- Ice cubes

Instructions:

1. Blend all ingredients until frothy.
2. Serve with a pineapple wedge garnish.

Thai Mango Coconut Smoothie

Ingredients:

- 1 cup ripe mango chunks
- 1/2 cup coconut milk
- 1/4 cup plain yogurt
- 1 tsp lime juice
- 1 tsp honey

Instructions:

1. Blend all ingredients until smooth.
2. Garnish with lime zest or a mint leaf.

Peruvian Lucuma Smoothie

Ingredients:

- 1/4 cup lucuma powder
- 1 banana
- 1/2 cup almond milk
- 1/4 cup plain yogurt
- 1 tsp vanilla extract
- Ice cubes

Instructions:

1. Blend all ingredients until creamy.
2. Serve with a sprinkle of lucuma powder on top.

Moroccan Orange and Date Smoothie

Ingredients:

- 1 orange, peeled and segmented
- 3 dates, pitted
- 1/2 cup almond milk
- 1/4 tsp cinnamon
- Ice cubes

Instructions:

1. Blend all ingredients until smooth.
2. Serve chilled with a sprinkle of cinnamon on top.

Italian Tiramisu Dessert Smoothie

Ingredients:

- 1/2 cup brewed espresso (cooled)
- 1/2 cup vanilla yogurt
- 1 frozen banana
- 1 tbsp mascarpone cheese
- 1 tbsp cocoa powder
- Ice cubes

Instructions:

1. Blend all ingredients until smooth.
2. Garnish with a dusting of cocoa powder and chocolate shavings.

Turkish Apricot and Almond Smoothie

Ingredients:

- 1/2 cup dried apricots, soaked
- 1/4 cup almond milk
- 1/4 cup plain yogurt
- 1 tbsp almond butter
- 1/2 tsp cinnamon
- Ice cubes

Instructions:

1. Blend all ingredients until smooth.
2. Serve with a sprinkle of chopped almonds on top.

Korean Banana Milk Smoothie

Ingredients:

- 1 banana
- 1/2 cup milk
- 1 tbsp sweetened condensed milk
- 1/4 tsp vanilla extract

Instructions:

1. Blend all ingredients until creamy.
2. Serve chilled with a banana slice on top.

French Lavender Blueberry Smoothie

Ingredients:

- 1/2 cup fresh or frozen blueberries
- 1/2 cup almond milk
- 1 tsp dried lavender flowers
- 1 tbsp honey
- Ice cubes

Instructions:

1. Heat the almond milk until warm and steep the lavender for 5 minutes, then strain.
2. Blend lavender-infused milk with blueberries, honey, and ice.
3. Serve chilled with a lavender sprig as garnish.

Hawaiian Tropical Papaya Smoothie

Ingredients:

- 1/2 cup papaya chunks
- 1/2 cup pineapple chunks
- 1/4 cup coconut milk
- 1/2 banana
- Ice cubes

Instructions:

1. Blend all ingredients until smooth.
2. Serve with a pineapple slice as garnish.

Spanish Almond Horchata Smoothie

Ingredients:

- 1/4 cup almonds, soaked
- 1/2 cup rice milk
- 1/4 tsp cinnamon
- 1 tbsp honey
- Ice cubes

Instructions:

1. Blend soaked almonds with rice milk, cinnamon, and honey until smooth.
2. Serve with a sprinkle of cinnamon on top.

Argentinian Dulce de Leche Smoothie

Ingredients:

- 2 tbsp dulce de leche
- 1/2 cup milk
- 1/4 cup vanilla yogurt
- 1/2 banana
- Ice cubes

Instructions:

1. Blend all ingredients until creamy.
2. Serve with a drizzle of dulce de leche on top.

Vietnamese Avocado Smoothie

Ingredients:

- 1 ripe avocado
- 1/2 cup condensed milk
- 1/2 cup coconut milk
- 1/4 tsp vanilla extract
- Ice cubes

Instructions:

1. Blend all ingredients until smooth and creamy.
2. Serve chilled, topped with crushed ice.

Swedish Lingonberry Smoothie

Ingredients:

- 1/2 cup lingonberries (fresh or frozen)
- 1/2 banana
- 1/2 cup plain yogurt
- 1/4 cup almond milk
- 1 tbsp honey
- Ice cubes

Instructions:

1. Blend all ingredients until smooth.
2. Serve chilled with a few lingonberries as garnish.

Ethiopian Spiced Honey Smoothie

Ingredients:

- 1/2 cup plain yogurt
- 1 tbsp honey
- 1/4 tsp cinnamon
- 1/4 tsp ground ginger
- 1/4 tsp ground cloves
- 1/2 cup water or almond milk
- Ice cubes

Instructions:

1. Blend all ingredients until smooth.
2. Serve with a sprinkle of cinnamon on top for garnish.

Lebanese Rosewater Pistachio Smoothie

Ingredients:

- 1/4 cup pistachios (soaked for 2 hours)
- 1/2 cup plain yogurt
- 1 tbsp rosewater
- 1/2 banana
- 1/2 cup almond milk
- 1 tbsp honey
- Ice cubes

Instructions:

1. Blend soaked pistachios, yogurt, rosewater, banana, almond milk, and honey until smooth.
2. Serve chilled, garnished with crushed pistachios.

Australian Beetroot and Carrot Smoothie

Ingredients:

- 1 small beetroot, peeled and chopped
- 1/2 carrot, peeled and chopped
- 1/2 cup orange juice
- 1/2 banana
- 1/4 cup almond milk
- Ice cubes

Instructions:

1. Blend all ingredients until smooth and vibrant.
2. Serve with a small slice of carrot or beetroot as garnish.

Filipino Ube (Purple Yam) Smoothie

Ingredients:

- 1/2 cup ube (purple yam) puree
- 1/2 banana
- 1/2 cup coconut milk
- 1 tbsp sweetened condensed milk
- Ice cubes

Instructions:

1. Blend all ingredients until smooth.
2. Serve chilled with a sprinkle of grated ube on top.

Chinese Lychee and Ginger Smoothie

Ingredients:

- 1/2 cup fresh or canned lychees, peeled
- 1/2 inch fresh ginger, peeled
- 1/2 cup coconut water
- 1/4 cup plain yogurt
- 1 tbsp honey
- Ice cubes

Instructions:

1. Blend all ingredients until smooth and fragrant.
2. Serve with a few whole lychees as garnish.

Russian Kefir Berry Smoothie

Ingredients:

- 1/2 cup kefir
- 1/2 cup mixed berries (strawberries, blueberries, raspberries)
- 1/2 banana
- 1 tbsp honey
- Ice cubes

Instructions:

1. Blend all ingredients until smooth and creamy.
2. Serve chilled, garnished with a few whole berries.

South African Rooibos Tea Smoothie

Ingredients:

- 1/2 cup brewed rooibos tea (cooled)
- 1/2 banana
- 1/4 cup coconut milk
- 1 tbsp honey
- Ice cubes

Instructions:

1. Brew rooibos tea and allow it to cool.
2. Blend cooled rooibos tea, banana, coconut milk, and honey until smooth.
3. Serve chilled with a sprig of mint as garnish.

Indonesian Tamarind and Coconut Smoothie

Ingredients:

- 2 tbsp tamarind pulp
- 1/2 cup coconut milk
- 1/2 banana
- 1 tbsp honey
- 1/4 tsp cinnamon
- Ice cubes

Instructions:

1. Blend tamarind pulp, coconut milk, banana, honey, and cinnamon until smooth.
2. Serve chilled with a slice of lime or coconut flakes as garnish.

Malaysian Pandan and Coconut Smoothie

Ingredients:

- 1/4 cup coconut milk
- 1/2 cup fresh coconut meat or shredded coconut
- 1 tbsp pandan extract
- 1/2 banana
- 1 tbsp honey or palm sugar
- Ice cubes

Instructions:

1. Blend coconut milk, coconut meat, pandan extract, banana, and honey until smooth.
2. Serve chilled with a sprinkle of shredded coconut on top.

Middle Eastern Date and Cardamom Smoothie

Ingredients:

- 4-5 pitted dates
- 1/2 tsp ground cardamom
- 1/2 cup plain yogurt
- 1/2 cup almond milk
- 1 tbsp honey
- Ice cubes

Instructions:

1. Blend dates, cardamom, yogurt, almond milk, and honey until smooth.
2. Serve chilled, garnished with a sprinkle of cardamom or chopped dates.

Colombian Passion Fruit Smoothie

Ingredients:

- 2-3 passion fruits, pulp scooped out
- 1/2 cup orange juice
- 1/2 banana
- 1 tbsp honey or sugar
- Ice cubes

Instructions:

1. Blend passion fruit pulp, orange juice, banana, and honey until smooth.
2. Serve chilled, garnished with extra passion fruit seeds for texture.

Swiss Chocolate Hazelnut Smoothie

Ingredients:

- 1/2 cup almond milk
- 1/2 banana
- 2 tbsp cocoa powder
- 2 tbsp hazelnut butter
- 1 tbsp honey or maple syrup
- Ice cubes

Instructions:

1. Blend almond milk, banana, cocoa powder, hazelnut butter, and honey until smooth.
2. Serve chilled with a drizzle of hazelnut butter on top.

Chilean Guava Smoothie

Ingredients:

- 1/2 cup guava pulp (fresh or frozen)
- 1/2 banana
- 1/2 cup coconut milk
- 1 tbsp honey
- Ice cubes

Instructions:

1. Blend guava pulp, banana, coconut milk, and honey until smooth.
2. Serve chilled, garnished with guava slices or mint leaves.

Polynesian Pineapple and Banana Smoothie

Ingredients:

- 1/2 cup pineapple chunks
- 1/2 banana
- 1/4 cup coconut milk
- 1/2 cup orange juice
- 1 tbsp honey
- Ice cubes

Instructions:

1. Blend pineapple, banana, coconut milk, orange juice, and honey until smooth.
2. Serve chilled with pineapple chunks or a slice of banana on top.

Danish Apple and Oat Smoothie

Ingredients:

- 1/2 apple, cored and chopped
- 1/4 cup rolled oats
- 1/2 cup almond milk
- 1 tbsp honey or maple syrup
- 1/2 tsp cinnamon
- Ice cubes

Instructions:

1. Blend apple, oats, almond milk, honey, and cinnamon until smooth.
2. Serve chilled with a sprinkle of cinnamon or oat flakes on top.

Finnish Cloudberry Smoothie

Ingredients:

- 1/2 cup cloudberries (fresh or frozen)
- 1/2 cup plain yogurt
- 1/4 cup apple juice
- 1 tbsp honey
- Ice cubes

Instructions:

1. Blend cloudberries, yogurt, apple juice, and honey until smooth.
2. Serve chilled, garnished with extra cloudberries or mint.

Indian Spiced Chai Smoothie

Ingredients:

- 1/2 cup brewed chai tea (cooled)
- 1/2 banana
- 1/4 cup plain yogurt
- 1/4 tsp ground cinnamon
- 1/4 tsp ground ginger
- 1 tbsp honey
- Ice cubes

Instructions:

1. Brew chai tea and allow it to cool.
2. Blend cooled tea, banana, yogurt, cinnamon, ginger, and honey until smooth.
3. Serve chilled with a cinnamon stick or star anise for garnish.

Tahitian Vanilla Coconut Smoothie

Ingredients:

- 1/2 cup coconut milk
- 1/2 cup plain yogurt
- 1 tbsp Tahitian vanilla extract
- 1/2 banana
- 1 tbsp honey
- Ice cubes

Instructions:

1. Blend coconut milk, yogurt, vanilla extract, banana, and honey until smooth.
2. Serve chilled with a sprinkle of shredded coconut for garnish.

Irish Cream and Coffee Smoothie

Ingredients:

- 1/2 cup brewed coffee (cooled)
- 1/4 cup Irish cream liqueur (optional for an alcoholic version)
- 1/2 banana
- 1 tbsp chocolate syrup
- 1/4 cup milk (or almond milk)
- Ice cubes

Instructions:

1. Blend coffee, Irish cream, banana, chocolate syrup, milk, and ice cubes until smooth.
2. Serve chilled with whipped cream and cocoa powder on top, if desired.

Jamaican Sorrel (Hibiscus) Smoothie

Ingredients:

- 1/2 cup sorrel (hibiscus) petals (fresh or dried)
- 1/2 cup water
- 1/2 cup pineapple juice
- 1 tbsp honey or sugar
- Ice cubes

Instructions:

1. Boil the sorrel petals in water for 10-15 minutes, then strain and cool.
2. Blend the cooled sorrel tea with pineapple juice, honey, and ice cubes until smooth.
3. Serve chilled with extra sorrel petals or a pineapple wedge for garnish.

Pakistani Almond and Saffron Smoothie

Ingredients:

- 1/4 cup almonds (soaked overnight)
- 1/2 cup milk
- 1/4 tsp saffron strands
- 1 tbsp honey
- 1/2 banana
- Ice cubes

Instructions:

1. Warm the milk slightly and steep the saffron strands in it.
2. Blend soaked almonds, saffron-infused milk, honey, banana, and ice cubes until smooth.
3. Serve chilled with a few whole almonds for garnish.

Ecuadorian Naranjilla Smoothie

Ingredients:

- 1/2 cup naranjilla pulp (fresh or frozen)
- 1/2 cup orange juice
- 1/4 cup pineapple juice
- 1 tbsp honey or sugar
- Ice cubes

Instructions:

1. Blend naranjilla pulp, orange juice, pineapple juice, honey, and ice cubes until smooth.
2. Serve chilled with an extra slice of orange or naranjilla fruit for garnish.

Icelandic Skyr Blueberry Smoothie

Ingredients:

- 1/2 cup Icelandic skyr (or plain yogurt as a substitute)
- 1/2 cup fresh or frozen blueberries
- 1/2 cup almond milk
- 1 tbsp honey or agave
- Ice cubes

Instructions:

1. Blend skyr, blueberries, almond milk, honey, and ice cubes until smooth.
2. Serve chilled with fresh blueberries or a mint leaf on top.

Cuban Guava and Cheese Smoothie

Ingredients:

- 1/2 cup guava paste or guava puree
- 1/4 cup cream cheese or ricotta cheese
- 1/4 cup coconut milk
- 1 tbsp honey
- Ice cubes

Instructions:

1. Blend guava paste, cream cheese, coconut milk, honey, and ice cubes until smooth.
2. Serve chilled with a few chunks of fresh guava for garnish.

Nigerian Zobo (Hibiscus) Smoothie

Ingredients:

- 1/2 cup dried hibiscus petals (zobo)
- 1/2 cup pineapple juice
- 1/4 cup water
- 1 tbsp honey or sugar
- Ice cubes

Instructions:

1. Boil the hibiscus petals in water for 10-15 minutes, then strain and cool.
2. Blend the cooled hibiscus tea with pineapple juice, honey, and ice cubes until smooth.
3. Serve chilled with a garnish of mint or hibiscus petals.

Alaskan Wildberry Smoothie

Ingredients:

- 1/2 cup wild blueberries (or mixed wildberries)
- 1/4 cup raspberries
- 1/2 banana
- 1/2 cup almond milk
- 1 tbsp honey or agave syrup
- Ice cubes

Instructions:

1. Blend wild blueberries, raspberries, banana, almond milk, honey, and ice cubes until smooth.
2. Serve chilled with extra wildberries for garnish.

Canadian Maple Apple Smoothie

Ingredients:

- 1/2 apple (peeled and cored)
- 1/2 cup unsweetened apple juice
- 1/2 cup plain yogurt
- 1 tbsp pure maple syrup
- 1/4 tsp ground cinnamon
- Ice cubes

Instructions:

1. Blend apple, apple juice, yogurt, maple syrup, cinnamon, and ice cubes until smooth.
2. Serve chilled with a drizzle of maple syrup or an apple slice for garnish.

Hungarian Sour Cherry Smoothie

Ingredients:

- 1/2 cup sour cherries (fresh or frozen)
- 1/2 cup plain yogurt
- 1/4 cup honey
- 1/4 cup water or almond milk
- Ice cubes

Instructions:

1. Blend sour cherries, yogurt, honey, water (or almond milk), and ice cubes until smooth.
2. Serve chilled with a few sour cherries on top for garnish.

Korean Sweet Potato Smoothie

Ingredients:

- 1/2 cooked sweet potato (peeled)
- 1/2 cup almond milk or oat milk
- 1/2 banana
- 1/2 tsp cinnamon
- 1 tbsp honey or maple syrup
- Ice cubes

Instructions:

1. Blend cooked sweet potato, almond milk, banana, cinnamon, honey, and ice cubes until smooth.
2. Serve chilled with a sprinkle of cinnamon on top.

Venezuelan Papelon con Limón Smoothie

Ingredients:

- 1/2 cup fresh lime juice
- 2 tbsp Venezuelan papelon (raw sugar cane) or brown sugar
- 1/2 cup water
- Ice cubes
- Lime slices for garnish

Instructions:

1. Dissolve papelon (sugar cane) in water, then mix with fresh lime juice.
2. Blend the sugar-lime water with ice cubes until smooth.
3. Serve chilled with a lime slice for garnish.

Balinese Turmeric and Tamarind Smoothie

Ingredients:

- 1/2 tsp ground turmeric
- 1 tbsp tamarind paste
- 1/2 banana
- 1/2 cup coconut water
- 1 tbsp honey
- Ice cubes

Instructions:

1. Blend turmeric, tamarind paste, banana, coconut water, honey, and ice cubes until smooth.
2. Serve chilled with a sprinkle of turmeric or a slice of lime.

Puerto Rican Pina Colada Smoothie

Ingredients:

- 1/2 cup pineapple chunks
- 1/2 cup coconut milk
- 1 tbsp shredded coconut
- 1/2 banana
- 1 tbsp honey or agave syrup
- Ice cubes

Instructions:

1. Blend pineapple chunks, coconut milk, shredded coconut, banana, honey, and ice cubes until smooth.
2. Serve chilled with a slice of pineapple or extra shredded coconut on top.

www.ingramcontent.com/pod-product-compliance
Lightning Source LLC
LaVergne TN
LVHW081339060526
838201LV00055B/2748